TRAVIS PASTRANA
MOTOCROSS SUPERSTAR

J. POOLOS

rosen central™

The Rosen Publishing Group, Inc., New York

Published in 2005 by The Rosen Publishing Group, Inc.
29 East 21st Street, New York, NY 10010

First Edition

Library of Congress Cataloging-in-Publication Data

Poolos, J.
Travis Pastrana : motocross superstar / by J. Poolos.
   p. cm.—(Extreme sports biographies)
Includes bibliographical references (p.   ) and index.
ISBN 1-4042-0071-1 (lib. bdg.)
1. Pastrana, Travis, 1983-—Juvenile literature. 2. Motorcyclists—United States—Biography—Juvenile literature. 3. Motocross—Juvenile literature. [1. Pastrana, Travis, 1983- 2. Motorcyclists. 3. Motocross.]
I. Title. II. Series: Extreme sports biographies (Rosen Publishing Group)
GV1060.2.P39P66 2004
796.7'5'092—dc22
                     2003023335

Manufactured in the United States of America

On the cover: Left: Travis Pastrana during the final round of the X Games motocross freestyle finals in August 2003, in Los Angeles, California. Right: Travis Pastrana at the 2001 X Games in Philadelphia, Pennsylvania.

CONTENTS

It is not death that a man should fear, but he should fear never beginning to live.

Marcus Aurelius, emperor of Rome, AD 121–180

Most of us don't like to be afraid. When we are faced with a particularly daunting challenge, we calculate our chances and either go for it or back off to reconsider. Weighing our options and determining the best approach helps make the challenge less frightening. Freestyle motocrosser and racer Travis Pastrana makes his living from these moments, from staring down fifteen-foot ramps and conquering his fear. As Travis told a reporter at alpinestars.com:

> I scare myself every day I get on a motorcycle. I think you'd have to be a complete idiot not to be frightened when you think you're going to crash. That doesn't change at all when you're a professional racer. Of course, the more you crash, the more ready you are. You try to prepare for a crash by getting yourself into better body position, but you still know it's going to hurt.

As a freestyle motocross superstar, Travis Pastrana faces his fears every day. Here, Travis watches the competition during the August 2002 X Games from the stands, thanks to an injured right leg.

Travis has had an amazing career so far, accomplishing feats others can only dream of. And he's done it with a great personality and a positive outlook on life and its challenges. Whether he's racing and jumping on his bike or hitting the books at school, his philosophy is consistent: "I just try to go out there and give it 110 percent every time," he said in a television interview after the 2003 X Games.

Travis's dedication and commitment are what enable him to pull off the amazing moves he performs. Here he celebrates after completing a 360-degree backflip during the motocross freestyle finals at the 2003 X Games.

CHAPTER ONE
LEARNING TO FLY

How would you like to ride a motorcycle up a ramp as high as the roof of a house, pull the handlebars back until you were upside down 50 feet (15 meters) above the ground, then finish the backflip and land on two wheels, 80 feet (24 m) from the point you took off? It may sound scary, but if you're Travis Pastrana, being scared is no big deal. Travis might do fifty jumps like this just warming up for a freestyle motocross competition. Freestyle motocross, or FMX, is a sporting event in which contestants jump motorcycles off huge ramps and do tricks while

In freestyle motocross, athletes perform tricks on motorcycles in midair. Here, Travis Pastrana competes in the freestyle motocross competition preliminaries at the 2003 Gravity Games in Cleveland, Ohio.

• •

flying through the air. Judges give points for each trick, based on difficulty, execution, and creativity. The rider with the most points wins the event.

Travis's athletic accomplishments are amazing. Among them are four X Games championships and one Gravity Games championship in freestyle motocross. In fact, he is undefeated in FMX competitions. He has invented many of the tricks that he and his fellow competitors use in contests. But he's not just a jumper. He's a racer, too. Between the ages of eight and fifteen, he won five National Amateur

Motocross Championships. After turning pro, he became the youngest rider ever to win a 125cc Supercross championship.

If you think Travis can't do anything but ride motorcycles, you're mistaken. He put in extra work in high school to graduate two years early and immediately enrolled at the University of Maryland.

What makes this kid tick? He is a motocrosser with a squeaky-clean image in a sport where most of the athletes sport tattoos and piercings and listen to heavy metal music. One of his rivals, Brian Deegan, is one such competitor. "Travis is the all-American kid," Deegan said in an interview in *Ultimate X—The Movie*, which documented X Games VII in 2001. "He's a role model for a certain group. But you got to have the good and bad to make the world go around—the positive and the negative. It's just the way it is. Pastrana is a good guy. Good for him. Deegan is a bad guy." He said of his band of riders who call themselves the Metal Mulisha, "It's a role model for a different group. The straight-A students can look up to Travis. The kid in detention can look up to the Mulisha."

Travis responds in the same interview, "The bottom line is that it all comes down to a respect thing between riders and what they can do on their motorcycles. In a way, I'm kind of the trendsetter, because when you win it doesn't

While Travis Pastrana projects an all-American image, fellow competitor and Metal Mulisha member Brian Deegan projects an edgier attitude. Shown here, Deegan attends the May 2002 premiere of ESPN's *Ultimate X—The Movie* in Universal City, California.

matter what you look like; there is kind of an automatic respect." To get to the bottom of who Travis is, it may help to look at what it was like for him growing up and at the two people who have made the biggest impression on him: his mother and father.

An Early Taste for Thrills

Travis Pastrana was born in Annapolis, Maryland, on October 8, 1983. His father, Robert, and his mother, Debbie, gave him a lot of freedom, even at an early age. You can get a glimpse of the kind of mother and father Travis's parents are in *Revelation 199*, a DVD showcasing Travis at home and at work on his bike. There is a good deal of video footage of Travis as a young child riding bicycles, go-karts, and minibikes.

In one scene, a three-year-old Travis is at the controls of a small bulldozer—not toy-small, but a real bulldozer used for small construction jobs. He's piloting it around the lot in front of Pastrana Construction while his father shouts out words of encouragement. Travis appears to be a well-schooled operator of this kind of equipment, but when wheeling the dozer around to drive it back to his father, he accidentally knocks over a 5-foot (1.5 m) section of concrete wall.

Many parents would have thrown a fit, but Travis's mother and father laugh heartily as the youngster drives the machine back toward them. "Travis," his father yells over the roar of the bulldozer, "was that good driving or bad driving?" When Travis just looks at him puzzled, he repeats the question, waiting patiently for the boy's response. This kind

Revelation 199 includes video footage of Travis as a young child and as a pro racer and jumper.

of nurturing, of using playtime to educate Travis, helped make him the kind of hero he is today.

But it wasn't just the nurturing that helped Travis become who he is. His parents' other qualities influenced him as well. Robert Pastrana is a bit of a risk taker. He was the kind of dad who would always jump off the high dive, and he'd encourage his young son to join him. Sure, Travis was afraid. But he trusted his father to take care of him. As

Travis at a Glance

Height/Weight: 6'2"/170 lbs.

Birth Date: October 8, 1983

Current Home: Davidson, Maryland

Originally From: Annapolis, Maryland

Favorite Sport (Besides MX): BMX dirt jumping

Favorite Musician: Jerry Lee Lewis

Hobbies: Skydiving, BMX, wakeboarding

Vehicles: Any Suzuki motorcycles, cars, or boats

Racing Number: 199

Classes: 125cc Supercross, 250cc Supercross

Year Turned Pro: 2000

a result, he developed confidence to overcome his fears. And he felt safe knowing he wouldn't be punished for making a mistake like wiping out on his bike.

In contrast to Robert, Debbie Pastrana is more reserved. She supports Travis in a different way. "Probably the biggest thing I can tell parents is to keep it fun," she told an interviewer in *Revelation 199*. "We never pushed [Travis], and we helped him . . . If he would get last [place], that was OK." While Robert showed Travis how to conquer his fears, Debbie showed him how to feel good about his accomplishments. She expressed her philosophy as a parent years later, shortly after Travis was injured in a warm-up for a competition, during an interview with Emily Badger of the *Cleveland Plain Dealer*:

> It's hard, it's very hard. Travis has broken over twenty bones and been in a wheelchair for two and a half months when they weren't sure if he would be paralyzed. It was the hardest thing as a parent, but you see your kid who tries and it's in their heart. As a parent, if you see this in your child, you have to support it. You have to. And if you don't support them, then lots of things are going to be worse. Because then they feel the friction of that and don't want to go against you. We are in it 100 percent, I've been with him every step of the way. When he's hurt and in rehab, he never complains, and that's when you know [that he's committed].

Travis's mother believes that if she did not support his motorcycle jumping, he wouldn't feel good about it, and that he needs to feel good about it in order to succeed and be safe. How cool is that?

Getting Started

Travis got his first minibike for Christmas when he was four years old. It was a 50cc model, which is a small bike suitable for beginners. He learned to ride in the yard and was soon racing around a small motocross track his dad had built on the family property. As Travis grew, he got a bigger minibike and began racing in local amateur races in the 80cc class.

Travis's Advice and Trivia

• Travis explains the best way to learn tricks: "Get a trampoline, take your bicycle, remove the wheels and cranks. Use some old rags on all sharp points with some duct tape . . . And you have yourself a freestyle learning device."

• Travis's longest jump ever is 207 feet (63 m)!

• In *Ultimate X*, Travis reveals that by age seventeen he had broken more than twenty-five bones and had undergone eight operations. "Hey, I'm only seventeen, but it's worth it," he said.

He won often, bringing home trophies taller than he was. Because he was so interested in racing, and because he was so good at it, his mother and father began taking him to races across the eastern seaboard. Success at these regional races led to races on the national level with the best amateur riders in the country, many of whom were older and more experienced than Travis. Parents of other racers and motorcycle industry people on the lookout for new talent spotted Travis as an up-and-comer, and he didn't let them down.

He placed second at the National Amateur Championship in 1991 in Hurricane Mills, Tennessee. That drew the attention of motorcycle manufacturer Suzuki, who made him the youngest factory-sponsored rider ever. From then on Travis would be given Suzuki motorcycles to race and travel expenses for competitions. He was eight years old.

This was the beginning of Travis's meteoric rise. He came in first at the 1992 National Amateur Motocross Championship and won again in 1993. When Travis had won five National Amateur Motocross Championships, he turned pro. As a professional racer, he could earn a salary from Suzuki and prize money for winning races. Suzuki would provide him with riding coaches, motorcycles, and equipment like helmets, boots, and pads. He would also be racing against the country's best riders.

Along the way he had become pretty good at doing tricks off of jumps. In fact, he found jumping a lot more fun than racing. But no one knew how successful he'd turn out to be as a jumper or how much he would change the sport of motorcycle jumping.

CAESARS PALACE

CHAPTER TWO
A BRIEF HISTORY OF MOTORCYCLE JUMPING

Ever since motorcycles were invented, riders have been jumping them. And ever since October 25, 1975, when millions of people tuned in to watch legendary daredevil Evel Knievel jump fourteen Greyhound buses at Kings Island near Cincinnati, Ohio, Americans have been excited about motorcycle jumping.

Knievel's stunts have been an inspiration to many young men and women, including Travis Pastrana. The creativity and engineering he used to set up his jumps—and the courage with which he executed them—were right

On December 31, 1967, Evel Knievel jumped over the fountain at Caesars Palace in Las Vegas, Nevada. He made the jump but crashed on landing and ended up in the hospital.

• •

up young Travis's alley. That was especially true of Knievel's epic jump across Idaho's Snake River Canyon in 1974 on a rocket-powered "Skycycle."

But early stunt shows began as less risky events, at least by our standards today. Even as late as the 1950s, it was common to hold automobile stunt shows between heats in stock car races. The most famous stunt driver was Joey Chitwood, whose Auto Daredevil Show featured Chitwood driving his car on two wheels or through a ring of fire, all at high speeds. Many young people saw his

thrilling show and were inspired to perform the same kind of feats themselves.

No one was more influenced by Joey Chitwood the daredevil than Evel Knievel, America's first motorcycle-jumping showman. And no other big-name jumper captured the public's attention like Knievel did. At a young age, he dreamed of doing the same kind of stunts to the applause of huge crowds. Not only did he put motorcycling on the map, he influenced the generations of jumpers that followed him.

Evel Captures America

Like Travis Pastrana, Evel Knievel was an active youth. Born Robert Craig Knievel in Butte, Montana, "Evel" was a champion ski jumper and later a semi-pro hockey player. After a short career as a racer, he began his stunt career in 1965. Between car races, he rode through walls of fire and jumped over live rattlesnakes and mountain lions. Later he began longer jumps over rows of cars. Knievel gained national prominence with his New Year's jump over the fountains at Caesar's Palace, a famous casino in Las Vegas, when he crashed horribly on landing. He was in a coma for thirty days and suffered many broken bones. But he made a big impression on the American public.

He kept jumping and drew record crowds for his death-defying feats. Along the way, he used the opportunity

Many people came to watch Evel Knievel's stunts. Here, he is lowered into a rocket-powered motorcycle for his attempt to jump the Snake River Canyon in 1974.

Selected Motocross Tricks

Every rider has his or her favorite tricks. Sometimes riders pull "combos," which are combinations of two or more tricks.

Can Can: One of the earliest tricks. Rider takes one foot off footpeg and raises leg up and over the seat so that both legs are on the same side of bike.

Whip: Rider "whips" the back end of the bike around at the peak of the jump and pushes the handlebars down sideways so the bike lies flat.

Heel Clicker: Rider raises feet above handlebars and wraps legs around arms, clicking heels together over the front fender.

Cliff-hanger: Rider lets go of handlebars and rises above the bike, catching the underside of the handgrips with the tops of feet. Raises hands up over head. (This trick is one of Travis's favorites.)

Cordova: Rider lifts feet under bars; hands still holding bars, brings knees to chest and arches back to look upside down over the back of the bike.

Fender Grab: Rider slides off the bike, keeping one hand on grip while the other grabs the rear fender.

Nothing: Rider pulls a no-footer (pulls feet off of the footpegs) and then takes hands from the handlebars.

Superman: Rider keeps hands on grips, takes feet from pegs and lies down flat on the bike, straightening arms to fly like Superman. Often combined with the seat grab.

Carey Hart performs his signature move, the Hart attack.

Hart Attack: Rider puts one hand on the seat, and with the other on the bars does a handstand. Named after inventor Carey Hart.

Bar Hop: Rider brings feet up between hands and over the handlebars so feet rest on the fender.

Saran Wrap: Rider places one leg between arms, then lifts one arm and swings leg around bars.

No Hands Lander: Rider lets go of handlebars in midair and lands the bike before grabbing the bars again.

Lazy Boy: Rider lets go of handlebar and lies down backward on the seat then extends feet past the handlebars. Invented by Travis Pastrana.

Backflip: The most hyped trick ever. Rider launches bike off ramp and leans back, pulling on the handlebars, so the bike somersaults backward.

360: Rider launches front wheel off of top corner of ramp, twisting the bike so it spins all the way around before landing. Hit for the first time at the 2003 X Games.

Evel Knievel's influence on extreme athletes is still felt today. Here, he is honored with a Pioneer Award at the ESPN Action Sports and Music Awards in Los Angeles, California.

to communicate messages that were important to him, such as encouraging kids to stay away from drugs. Knievel retired an American hero. He was so famous that his motorcycle, jumpsuit, and other memorabilia are on display at the Smithsonian Institute's Museum of American History in Washington, D.C.

There were motorcycle jumpers who followed, but none was as famous as Evel Knievel. Then motorcycle technology advanced and changed the sport even more. In an effort to improve the handling of racing motorcycles, engineers at motorcycle manufacturers developed shock absorbers that could withstand the force of high jumps and sharp bumps. It was a meaningful breakthrough for racers, and it made it possible for the next crop of jumpers to break new ground. Soon the designers of motocross courses began to make the jumps bigger and more challenging. Riders began jumping farther than ever. Some did tricks, like taking a foot off of the footpeg or their hands off of the handlebars in midair.

Travis Learns to Jump

Travis began jumping at a very young age, and by age ten he was already jumping off of full-size motocross jumps. He and his dad built an ever-growing series of long, winding tracks that run all through the woods behind their house. Travis made sure there were plenty of jumps where he could practice the tricks he had seen other motocross riders perform. And practice he did. In *Revelation 199*, he can be seen learning the art of jumping. He can also be seen learning the art of falling.

But the more Travis practiced, the better he got. Once he mastered the 10-foot (3 m) jumps, he tried bigger jumps. He added tricks to his jumps, and it wasn't long before he was sailing 50 feet (15 m) through the air doing tricks like the whip and nac-nac. Travis was coming into his own at the right time, for it was then that the whole motorcycle world was about to become mesmerized by a new form of motocross: freeriding.

CHAPTER THREE
THE BIRTH OF FREESTYLE MOTOCROSS

Freeriding, a term used to describe riding and jumping in an open area rather than racing on a track or course, has been a popular activity for a long time. During motocross races, riders who were too far back to place well would pull tricks off of jumps to entertain the crowds. Eventually, some people decided it would be fun to jump outside of the racing environment. In the early 1990s, freeriding caught the attention of the media. Motocross magazines began to describe the creative and awesome tricks freeriders performed as "freestyle." Incidentally, most of these tricks

Motocross riders, including Kyle McCutcheon *(right)*, take a jump during a 125 expert class competition at the September 2003 Otero County Motocross Association race in Tularosa, New Mexico.

• •

were first performed on BMX bikes in the 1980s and were made famous in BMX video documentaries in the 1990s.

Then the dam broke. In 1994, two filmmakers got together and began shooting footage for a film about the lifestyle of a typical pro motocross rider. Jon Freeman and Dana Nicholson, each known for shooting extreme sports action such as snowboarding and surfing, had already made many well-known snowboarding videos. They also made *In Black and White*, a brilliant action documentary centered on Kelly Slater, one of the world's most dynamic surfers. Freeman and Nicholson now turned to the young men who rode through the deserts and in the mountains and woods, performing amazing feats on motocross bikes.

What caught the attention of the filmmakers was something they had never seen before. When training, the riders often soared off of huge jumps. Soon this became the focus of the movie. These riders thought nothing of jumping 145 feet (44 m), soaring 45 feet (14 m) off the ground. They would jump over anything: sand dunes, mountains, houses, buses, and more. The filmmakers infused their footage with heavy metal and rap music. The result was the well-known video *Crusty Demons of Dirt*, released by Fleshwound Films in 1995.

No one could have predicted the impact this video would have on the world of sports. According to the Fleshwound Films Web site, "The excitement and hysteria the film created was phenomenal." People had never seen anything like the stunts these guys were doing. Because the modern motocross bikes allowed them to jump farther and higher than ever before, they made Evel Knievel's jumps look like child's play. But the film also captured the essence of this lifestyle, the zaniness and "go-for-it" attitude, much in the same way *Endless Summer* and *On Any Sunday* did in the 1960s and 1970s for surfing and motorcycle riding, respectively. It mixed heavy metal and rap soundtracks with a seemingly endless stream of jaw-dropping stunts. *Crusty* became a cult phenomenon.

Crusty Demons of Dirt 2 was released eighteen months later, and the extreme jumping videos began to draw a

Motocross Competitions

There are two main motocross championships in the United States and several worldwide. The indoor series is currently called the EA Sports AMA Supercross Series. The outdoor series is called the AMA/Chevy Trucks U.S. Motocross Championship. The American Motorcycle Association (AMA) sanctions both series, and many of the same riders appear in both.

The indoor series runs from January to May. The outdoor series runs from May through August. Each series comprises a number of rounds, usually twelve to fifteen. Each round is run over a weekend in a different U.S. city and features qualifying heats and two "mains," or races for points. All qualifiers participate in both mains. Points are awarded based on how a rider places in each main. At the end of the season, the rider with the most points wins the championship.

large international audience. The videos influenced thousands of young people, who went out and bought bikes to jump or began jumping those they had. After *Crusty Demons of Dirt 3* was released in 1997, two people who were important for the heightened popularity of freeriding had the idea to hold a freestyle competition. This competition was held in Las Vegas. Many in the extreme sports scene thought that turning what was essentially a laidback jam session into a winner/loser scenario was a bad idea. But fan appreciation and enthusiasm were tremendous, and the doubters were soon silenced.

The 1995 film *Crusty Demons of Dirt* had an enormous impact on the growth of the popularity of the sport of motocross. In this photo, Dayne Kinnaird struts his stuff at the Rod Laver Arena in Melbourne, Australia, during the Crusty Demons of Dirt Global Assault Tour in May 2003.

Freestyle Gets Organized

The popularity of freestyle competitions led to the formation of the International Freestyle Motocross Association (IFMA) in 1998. The organization was formed to sanction events and create an annual world championship. Meanwhile, the extreme sports culture was on the rise. Sports like skateboarding, BMX, and snowboarding had become more popular than ever, and people outside of the younger generation were beginning to take notice. No one was more important to the future of extreme sports than one influential programming executive at a well-known television network.

In 1993, Ron Semiao, then director of programming at the television network ESPN, recognized the potential popularity of alternative sports. He thought a meeting of athletes from different extreme sports could create great exposure for ESPN, as well as for the athletes and their sports. He and the creative minds at ESPN began to plan a huge competitive gathering of extreme sports athletes. In 1995, the first Extreme Games were held in Rhode Island. Featured sports included skateboarding, BMX, and street luge. The games were an outrageous success, drawing nearly 200,000 spectators.

In 1996, the name was changed to the X Games, and a Winter X Games was added. In addition to snowboarding events, there was snow mountain-bike racing, ice climbing, and shovel racing. As years went by, the games became more refined and more popular. The games featured cool music and alternative fashion to create a hip, edgy atmosphere. At the X Games, the emphasis is on the individual, not on the team.

In 1999, motocross events were introduced to the X Games in San Francisco. Riders competed in freestyle jumping and doubles jumping. That year, freestyle motocross, thought of as the extreme of extremes, attracted more spectators than any other event at the X Games. Eventually, doubles jumping was dropped in favor of "big air" and the "step up." But freestyle jumping continues to be the favored

Travis Pastrana is captured midrace during the February 2002 EA Sports AMA Supercross Series at Edison International Field in Anaheim, California.

event. This is due in no small part to the amazing talents of Travis Pastrana, who steals the show every time by thrilling the crowds with creative tricks and flawless technique.

Today, freestyle motocross is a featured event at the second largest extreme sports competition, the Gravity Games, and in major demonstrations. It is also featured as a daily performance at Disneyland, featuring none other than the Godfather of Freestyle, Mike Metzger.

Mike Metzger executes a motocross stunt over a replica of the Golden Gate Bridge for the opening of Disney's X Games Experience in California. Outrageous stunts such as these are what make the sport so popular.

Carey Hart, the first rider to land a backflip in competition, comments on the sudden popularity of freestyle motocross in *Ultimate X*: "People now definitely know we're athletes and not just daredevils throwing ourselves all over the place, and it takes a lot of technique and a lot of style to do the things that we're doing." In the same interview, Travis weighed in on the subject: "The X Games is without a doubt the biggest event in freestyle and any other extreme sports."

CHAPTER FOUR
TRAVIS GOES BIG

In 1999, the year freestyle motocross was added to the X Games, fifteen-year-old Travis wheeled his Suzuki into the FMX stadium in San Francisco and made history. His competitors were aware of his talents. He had already won several freestyle contests, including the Free Air Festival events in Las Vegas and Tacoma, Washington, in 1998. Earlier in the year, he had won his fifth amateur national championship in motocross. He had then turned professional just in time to enter the last race of the World Supercross Series. There, he charged from the back of the

Travis Pastrana was fifteen when he stunned the extreme sports world by winning a gold medal in his first professional competition.

• •

pack to take the win in his first professional race. It was a huge accomplishment for the budding professional racer. The seeds of his legend had been sown. Now he was about to make his mark on America.

Travis had ridden well in the qualifying round. Now it was showtime. The moments before the final round were intense. All the qualifiers were top-notch. Mike Metzger and Brian Deegan put on exceptional performances, thrilling the screaming crowds with trick after trick—whips, heel clickers, and Hart attacks. But Travis rewrote the book. He displayed

Freestyle Events

The X Games has three events for motorcycles. Each are scored separately. Gold, silver, and bronze medals are awarded in each event.

FMX: Each rider has ninety seconds to do as many tricks as possible on a course with jumps of different sizes. Typically a rider can do ten jumps in this time period.

Big Air: Riders go off the biggest ramp on the course and hit a trick or a combination of tricks. Judges award points for each jump. The best score of three jumps is taken, and the rider with the highest score wins.

Step Up: Riders motor up a steep ramp and turn their bikes sideways, parallel to the ground, to clear a bar. Riders who don't clear the bar are eliminated. After each round the bar is raised. The rider who clears the greatest height wins.

a masterful use of the course on his way to a first-round score of 99 (out of 100). His routine was awesome: he hit a giant Superman, a no-handed heel click, and two no-hands landings. He also busted out a soaring no-handed seat grab that was simply spectacular.

His heel clickers were crisp and well timed. The extension of his scissor kicks made him look relaxed, like all of this was no big deal for him. He seemed to defy gravity. The crowed loved him. And at the end of his routine, he pulled out all the stops. He rode around a jump, aimed for another, and pinned the throttle, launching his bike out of the stadium and straight into San Francisco Bay.

It is safe to say that no one in attendance had ever seen anything like it. Here was this fifteen-year-old, clean-cut kid from Maryland, the youngest of the competitors, having just proven he was in his own league as a jumper, launching his bike off of a giant ramp and disappearing into the bay. How extreme is that? The crowd went wild. Travis surfaced, pumped his fist into the air, and climbed up on the shore, where his father was waiting, clad in a life vest. Needless to say, Travis brought home the gold and in the same breath sealed his fate as a wild man.

Travis told a reporter in *Ultimate X*: "Since it was on my last run and it wouldn't hold up the competition, I decided to do it." His antics made national news, although much to the disappointment of his new following, ESPN refused to air the jump into the bay for fear that outcries from environmentalists would tarnish the image of the X Games. Travis was fined $10,000 for the stunt, his entire winnings from the competition.

A Breakout Year

His fellow competitors were fantastic performers, but it was Travis who put FMX on the map. But he didn't stop there. In September of that year, Travis won the NBC Gravity Games in Rhode Island with an outstanding final run. He and training partner Kenny "Cowboy" Bartram took home gold medals in the doubles competition.

On November 11, 1999, Travis was invited to appear on *The Late Show with David Letterman*. He had set up a ramp on 53rd Street outside the Ed Sullivan Theater in New York City. But during rehearsal, he crashed on landing, slightly injuring himself. The show aired some of his practice jumps, thrilling live crowds and the television audience alike. Letterman introduced him as "an amazing athlete."

That year had its share of highlights. But 2000 was a phenomenal breakout year for Travis. When it came time to race, he began his first full year as a pro with great success. He had some strong performances during the first two months of the indoor season. Then, in March, he won the AMA Supercross 125 races in Daytona Beach, Florida, and St. Louis, Missouri. He added a win later in the year, battling eventual champion Stephane Roncada for the championship. But Travis lacked the experience to win consistently, and he wound up the season in a solid third place.

When the Supercross Series was over, the national outdoor series began. Travis again battled Roncada for the championship. Travis had learned a lot during the Supercross season, and he was riding smoother and faster than ever. Near the end of the series, he began a long winning streak, winning five mains in a row. At the last round, he was sixty-five points behind Roncada in the series. But he stormed through the final heat to win the championship by only two points and end his winning streak at seven motos. It was his first championship as a professional rider. He was the youngest AMA champion ever.

In recognition of his progress and of his outstanding performance, he was named AMA Rookie of the Year. "I was the youngest person ever to win the 125cc championship," Travis told a reporter from *Racer X* magazine. "It's

Stephane Roncada is just one of the group of talented riders who compete with Travis Pastrana. In this photo, Roncada races during the 2002 EA Sports AMA Supercross Series at Edison International Field in Anaheim, California.

just an amazing feeling to break a record. It was a day I'll never forget, and hopefully this year I'll be able to take the title again."

But the excitement had only just begun. After the outdoor motocross series, Travis was named the youngest member ever to the U.S. team in the prestigious Motocross des Nations. This event has an interesting format. Three-person teams consisting of the best motocross

Ricky Carmichael takes a tight corner during the 1999 AMA/Chevy Trucks National Motocross Series at Glen Helen Raceway in San Bernardino, California. Carmichael was one of Travis Pastrana's team-mates in the 2000 Motocross des Nations race.

racers from countries all over the world compete in three races. Each team has a rider on a 125cc motorcycle, one on a 250cc motorcycle, and one on a 500cc motorcycle. Each class of motorcycle is pitted against another. Points are awarded separately for each class based on the order of finish. So, for example, when the 125cc class races with the 500cc class, the first 125cc rider to cross the finish line earns first place, and the first 500cc motorcycle to cross the finish line earns a win, too. After all of the races have been run, overall winners are named from each class.

Competition was fierce, and it was tough riding on the track with the bigger, faster motorcycles of his competitors. But Travis prevailed, winning the 125cc class. His team-mates, Ricky Carmichael and Ryan Hughes, won their classes as well, sweeping the field and bringing the prestigious Motocross des Nations trophy back to the United States. Travis was on a roll.

CHAPTER FIVE
ON TOP OF THE WORLD

After the Motocross des Nations, Travis made his way to San Francisco for the 2000 X Games. Once again, Travis was the toast of the town. He was so confident with his qualifying run that at the end of it he attempted a backflip, a trick that had never yet been done. Halfway through he decided he wouldn't make it all the way around and bailed out. During the final round, Travis again proved he was a cut above the rest, stringing together a run of artful tricks and earning a score of 94. Tommy Clowers was second, and Brian Deegan was third.

Travis Pastrana made his mark in the sport by taking chances. Here, he leaps off his motorcycle during a jump at the motocross freestyle competition at the 2000 ESPN X Games in San Francisco, California.

Travis began the 2001 motocross season with all the momentum that comes with winning a championship, a prestigious international race, and an X Games gold medal. Suzuki, his sponsor, had promoted him to the 250cc class. This meant faster machines and more experienced riders. Travis quickly realized he hadn't yet developed the physical strength necessary to wrestle the bigger motorcycles around the track, so he traded his 250cc ride for a 125cc motorcycle and entered the Eastern Regional Supercross Series. Again, Travis force. In the seven races he entered, he won five, scoring enough points to win the championship.

But the outdoor season was a different story. Compared to the previous year, Travis came out of the gates slowly. It wasn't until the fourth event that he won a race. And throughout the first half of the season, he experienced several hard crashes. As a result, he suffered nagging injuries that eventually forced him to make a tough decision. He could keep racing and suffer with pain, mediocre results, and risk of further injury, or he could take a break from racing and give his injuries time to heal. He chose to withdraw from the series and cut back on his training on a temporary basis. It was hard for the budding superstar to stand by while his competitors continued to race, especially when it seemed everything had been going so well.

Back in Competition, Believe It or Not

By the time the Summer X Games rolled around, Travis was healthy, but he hadn't competed in a freestyle event in a long time. As the competitors arrived in Philadelphia, many riders and fans didn't think Travis could win against those who had jumped throughout the year. Brian Deegan, who had never won an X Games gold medal in freestyle, saw this as his best chance yet to show up the clean-cut Pastrana. But after Travis's first qualifying run, it was clear to all that he was on top of his game, while crowd-favorite Deegan ran into some trouble during his qualifying run. He overshot a landing and rode his bike into a padded barrier, knocking it over on top of a half-dozen cameramen who were standing behind it. "I just lost my mind for a minute and took out a bunch of people," the bad boy of FMX said in *Ultimate X*.

Deegan's troubles continued in the final round. He hit all of his jumps, but his performance lacked its usual precision and flair. After the run, he commented on his sub-par performance. "That's the lamest scoring I've ever got, the worst I've ever ridden. But guess what? I had fun," he told *Ultimate X*.

Tommy Clowers had an outstanding run that put him in first place. Alternate Jake Windham beat Clowers's score with smooth, consistent riding. Windham earned a spot in the event when Jeremy Carter crashed out in practice, break-ing both legs and knocking out some teeth. Next came Clifford Adoptante, who ripped a spectacular run that had the crowd on their feet. His score topped Windham's with only Travis left to ride.

A reporter from *Ultimate X* asked Travis before the event if he ever gets nervous before a freestyle competition. Travis replied, "I've never actually lost a freestyle motocross event, and yes, it's kind of something I do just to go out and have a lot of fun. So I fcel a little bit of pressure—but mostly just pressure I put on myself to do all my tricks the best that I can possibly do them."

Travis opened the run with style. He started from the rider's area, rode down the runway, hit the biggest jump in fourth gear, and nailed a Superman seat grab Indian air combination. Again, he thrilled the crowds with an arsenal of perfectly executed tricks and flawless landings, earning a score of 96.33 and his third straight X Games gold medal. Clifford Adoptante earned the silver medal and Jake

45

Windham the bronze medal. It was an exciting contest with phenomenal riding from the top riders.

Later that year, Travis took some time off to fulfill a life-long dream. On November 14, he jumped his Suzuki into the Grand Canyon. He had planned every last detail of the stunt—including extensive skydiving lessons—and he was confident he could do it safely. His mother and father accompanied him to Arizona, along with a small crew and cameramen from the television show *Ripley's Believe It or Not*. Travis first jumped the bike into the canyon in a practice run. He gave his parents a scare when he barely cleared the cliff after jumping off the ramp. For his second jump, he pinned the throttle in fourth gear, hit the ramp, pulled a back-flip, then ditched the bike and parachuted into the 2,000-foot (610-m) gorge. When asked by a reporter at ESPN.com why he did a backflip into the Grand Canyon, Travis replied, "Heck, since I was about ten years old I wanted to jump it. Every motocrosser in the world thinks about it."

Motocross Personalities

Travis gets to compete against an interesting and varied group of riders. Here are mini-biographies on some of them.

Mike Metzger

Nickname: The Godfather. Born: Huntington Beach, California. Birthdate: November 19, 1975. Height: 5'10". Weight: 150 lbs. Hometown: Menifee, California.

Known as the Godfather of Freestyle, Mike is considered one of the pioneers of the sport. He won the 2002 X Games by sticking two consecutive backflips. He has been part of

Tommy Clowers is just one of the personalities that make up the sport of motocross. Here, Tom Cat, as he is known, performs a rockin' stunt at the 2002 X Games at First Union Center in Philadelphia, Pennsylvania.

Disneyland's FMX show, where he does four performances a day. He missed the 2003 X Games due to an injury suffered in training.

Brian Deegan

Born: Omaha, Nebraska. Birthdate: May 9, 1975. Height: 5'9". Weight: 170 lbs. Hometown: Temecula, California.

Deegan is one of the most influential riders in FMX. He is part of the Metal Mulisha, a group of alternative FMX riders.

Whether he's winning or losing, bad boy Brian Deegan has fun during competitions. Here, he's captured in the middle of performing a Hart attack during the motocross competition at the 2001 Winter X Games.

He holds more X Games medals than any other rider. He is the first rider to do a 360 in competition.

Tommy Clowers

Nickname: Tom Cat. Born: San Diego, California. Birthdate: September 2, 1972. Height: 5'5". Weight: 155 lbs. Hometown: Ramona, California.

Tommy is one of the most versatile and best all-around riders ever. He won three straight gold medals in the X Games step up and has taken medals in the Winter X Games as well.

Nate Adams

Nickname: Nate Dog. Born: Glendale, Arizona. Birthdate: March 29, 1984. Height: 6'. Weight: 165 lbs. Hometown: Wittmann, Arizona.

Nate is considered by many FMX riders to have the best form of any jumper around. Yet he has remained out of the medal running in major competitions—until X Games 2003, where he earned a silver medal. He was the first to nail a backflip no-hands lander in competition.

Kenny Bartram

Nickname: Cowboy. Born: Stillwater, Oklahoma. Birthdate: August 23, 1978. Height: 6'. Weight: 170 lbs. Hometown: Stillwater, Oklahoma.

Kenny has a huge bag of tricks, and he's not afraid to go big. He has the reputation as a dedicated rider who goes for it at every jump. He was the first to land a backflip heel clicker in competition.

Carey Hart

Nickname: Vegas. Born: Las Vegas, Nevada. Birthdate: July 17, 1975. Height: 5'11". Weight: 170 lbs. Hometown: Las Vegas, Nevada.

Carey is most famous for being the first rider to ever attempt the backflip in a competition at the 2000 Gravity Games. Two years later, he hit it for the first time at the 2002 X Games, where he won a silver medal.

CHAPTER SIX
OVERCOMING SETBACKS

T ravis raced Supercross again in 2002, giving the 250cc class another shot. After several races with consistently high finishes, including a second place at the San Diego round, it looked like the season was shaping up for a more mature Travis. He was riding more consistently than ever, and Suzuki's hopes were high that its rider would finish a lot of races on the winner's podium.

But Travis suffered a concussion after a crash. And at the Daytona round, weak with the flu, Travis pulled off the track during the race and passed out. Shortly after that

Despite many setbacks, Travis Pastrana went on to place first in the freestyle motocross finals at the 2002 Gravity Games in Cleveland, Ohio. Here he is performing a backflip.

incident, he had surgery to correct chronic sinusitis, making it easier for him to breathe through his nose. At this time he also came down with weakening viral infections, including the Epstein-Barr virus and mononucleosis. With his hopes of placing high in the Supercross series dashed, Travis could only look forward to the Gravity Games freestyle event in January.

When the Gravity Games came around, Travis was ready with his backflip. He and Mike Metzger were the only riders there who could do the trick consistently. The judges awarded a lot of points for the backflip, so the other competitors could only fight for the bronze medal, as Travis won the gold and Mike won the silver. In what some at the time called the most amazing freestyle run ever, Travis nailed seven backflips, once again wowing the crowd. But during the step up competition, Travis landed too far forward and plummeted 30 feet (9 m) to the ground, seriously injuring his knee. Four months later, he had recovered and was ready for the 2003 Supercross series. But in the season opener at Glen Helen, in San Bernadino, California, he suffered a season-ending knee injury. Once again, Travis was sidelined.

It was a trying time for Travis. His string of injuries and illnesses seemed never-ending. He decided to sit out the outdoor motocross nationals and rest his body. The naturally active Travis found life without racing and jumping frustrating. Then something happened that would change his life forever.

Late one night, Travis and a friend were involved in an automobile accident. His friend suffered a broken back and temporary paralysis. Travis was devastated and wrote a letter to the editors of *Racer X* magazine to explain the circumstances. *Racer X* published the letter. "In the past month, without a set training schedule and without the

A knee injury sidelined Travis from competition for much of 2003. That didn't stop him from attending motocross events to cheer on his friends and competitors.

excitement of racing, I have been waking up in the middle of the night to drive my car," he stated in the letter. He then explained that he had been driving too fast in a rural area when a deer ran onto the road. "We were in the woods before I knew what had happened, and my friend is still in the hospital because I drove too fast. I never thought it would happen and still can't believe it did, but I have never been more sorry in my entire life." It was a difficult lesson for Travis to learn, but he realized he had to act more responsibly and save his risk-taking for the track.

In mid-summer of 2003, Travis didn't think he would be healthy enough to compete in the X Games, but he did some training in his new foam pit, which allowed him to practice tricks safely—especially new tricks. The pit is like a swimming pool filled with foam blocks. When August arrived, he was ready to go.

The 360

In August 2003, the X Games IX arrived with tons of excitement for the motocross freestyle competitors and fans. By this time, FMX had grown so popular, it drew more fans than any other X Games event. The daredevils were always inventing new tricks to push the limits. The 2002 X Games were all about the backflip. Now everyone wondered what the next amazing trick would be.

More than 40,000 screaming fans packed the Los Angeles Coliseum for the main event. The Metal Mulisha's Brian Deegan came into the final round having scored the most points in the preliminary round. Travis had the second most points, setting up a classic duel of "good versus evil." But they weren't the only two who rode strong in the preliminary round. Other favorites included Kenny Bartram and Nate Adams. About half the riders had hit backflips, but no one had pulled any new tricks that rivaled the buzz the backflip had created the year before.

Deegan was the first of the favorites to jump. He was on top of his game and put in a strong run. For his last jump, he did a trick that had never been attempted before in competition: a 360. The idea was to take off from the top of the ramp and spin the motorcycle 360 degrees before landing. Deegan landed almost perfectly sideways on the downside of the ramp, not quite able to spin the bike all the way around. But he straightened it out and saved it. The crowd and the announcers went crazy. Deegan had raised the bar. Now everyone would have to pull out all the stops.

When it was Travis's turn, he started off with a monster backflip over the 87-foot (26.5 m) gap, then over the second jump he hit a fully extended kiss of death. He was only ten seconds into his routine and he had already cast a spell on the crowd. They knew something big was going to happen if Travis was going to keep his undefeated streak alive in freestyle.

He pulled more tricks, including an awesome no-foot backflip. Near the end of his run, he rode slowly around the outside of the arena, standing on the footpegs and gesturing to the crowd to pump up the volume. Then he blasted off toward a ramp at an angle and went off the lip, pushing his foot against the bike and whipping the back end around. He, too, had hit a 360, and he rotated his bike all the way around. But when he landed, he fell off the back of the motorcycle.

Travis celebrates a winning performance after the motocross freestyle competition at the 2003 X Games in Los Angeles, California.

The noise level in the coliseum was deafening. Travis jumped up and ran over to his fallen motorcycle with his arms raised over his head, pumping up the crowd even more. He got on his bike and headed off to the ramp again. He tried another 360, and this time he nailed the landing. The fans were rabid. The cheers lasted a full five minutes after his run had finished. "I didn't want to do that trick," Travis said of the 360, "but Deegan came out and did it. All the props out to Brian for doing it. Once he did the trick, I was like, 'Now I have to do it,'" he told *Racer X*. The judges put Travis in first, just ahead of Deegan.

The last competitor was Nate Adams. Nate didn't attempt a 360, but his run showcased his wide variety of tricks, including the no hands backflip and the backflip heel clicker, as well as perfect execution. His score was enough to push Deegan to third but not enough to take first from Travis. "I'm telling you, Nate Adams has by far the best arsenal of tricks in the world," Travis told *Racer X*. "I knew without the 360 that there was no possible way in the world that my tricks would be half as good as his."

But it was Travis who won the gold medal and remained undefeated in freestyle. "There have been a lot of setbacks here recently," Travis told *Racer X*, describing his year. "So it was really nice to win again."

What's next for Travis? Right now, he has a lot of options. Because of his injuries and the wear and tear the sport takes on the body, he's not sure if he'll continue to race motocross. If he doesn't, he'd like to race rally cars. He also plans to continue working toward his college degree and to eventually get into broadcasting. Whatever he does, you can bet he'll do it with flair. As he said to a writer in an internet chat room, "The most important thing for me is to work hard and try to be the best person I can be. As long as I do that, I'll always be happy with myself."

GLOSSARY

BMX Bicycle motocross.

cc (cubic centimeter) A unit of measurement used to describe the size of the engine in the motor-cycle industry.

daredevil A recklessly bold person.

documentary A film that describes a real event or person.

FMX Freestyle motocross; the sporting event in which contestants on motorcycles jump and perform tricks.

heat One of several preliminary races held to eliminate less competent contenders.

kiss of death A trick in which the rider takes his or her feet off the footpegs and fully extends his or her body over the back of the bike, putting his or her face to the handlebars while looking upward.

memorabilia Things that are worthy of remembrance.

minibike A small motorcycle, usually used by kids.

moto One of two races in which riders earn champi-onship points.

nac-nac A trick executed by taking one leg off the foot-peg and swinging it over the seat and rear fender, extending it back.

pin the throttle To open the throttle all the way.

stunt shows An unusual or difficult feat requiring great skill or daring, done to gain public attention.

Superman seat grab Indian air A Superman trick in which the rider lets go with one hand and grabs the seat while doing a scissors kick with his or her legs.

American Motorcyclist Association
Motorcycle Hall of Fame Museum
13515 Yarmouth Drive
Pickerington, OH 43147
(614) 856-2222
Web site: http://www.amadirectlink.com

Racer X Illustrated
166 Harner Run
Morgantown, WV 26508
(304) 284-0080
Web site: http://www.racerxill.com

Women's Motocross Association
22975 Nelson Road
Bend, OR 97701
(541) 317-0636
Web site: http://www.womensmotocrossassociation.com

Web Sites

Due to the changing nature of Internet links, the Rosen
Publishing Group, Inc., has developed an online list of
Web sites related to the subject of this book. This site is
updated regularly. Please use this link to access the list:

http://www.rosenlinks.com/exb/tpas

FOR FURTHER READING

Bales, Donnie, and Gary Semics. *Pro Motocross and Off-Road Motorcycle Techniques*. Osceola, WI: Motorbooks International, 2001.

Collins, Ace. *Evel Knievel: An American Hero*. New York: St. Martin's Press, 1999.

Coombs, Davey, and Eric Johnson. *American Motocross Illustrated*. Morgan Hill, CA: Fox Racing, 2002.

Milan, Garth, and Donnie Bales. *Freestyle Motocross: Jump Tricks from the Pros*. 2nd edition. Osceola, WI: Motorbooks International, 2000.

Ryan, Ray. *Motocross Racers: 30 Years of Legendary Dirt Bikes*. Osceola, WI: Motorbooks International, 2001.

Savage, Jeff. *Supercross Motorcycle Racing*. Englewood Cliffs, NJ: Silver Burdett Press, 1996.

BIBLIOGRAPHY

Badger, Emily. "Mom's Heart Turns with Every Backflip." *Cleveland Plain Dealer*, August 4, 2002.

Bartoldus, Erick. "Catching Up with Travis Pastrana." March 19, 2003. Retrieved August 18, 2003 (http://www.transworldmotocross.com/mx/interview/article/0,13190,343607,00.html).

Bartoldus, Erick. "Travis Pastrana: On the Right Track." January 18, 2002. Retrieved August 11, 2003 (http://www.transworldmotocross.com/mx/features/article/0,13190,343745,00.html).

Coombs, Davey. *MX: The Way of the Motocrosser*. New York: Harry N. Abrams, 2003.

Gordon, Devin. "Up, Up, and Away, Dude! Extreme Sports." *Newsweek,* January 2000, pp. 26,78.

Graveline, Eddie. "Five Minutes with Travis Pastrana." January 5, 2000. Retrieved August 3, 2003 (http://www.motopress.net/main/riders/travispastrana.htm).

Maeda, Donn. "Catching Up with Travis Pastrana." February 7, 2001. Retrieved August 18, 2003 (http://www.transworldmotocross.com/mx/interview/article/0,13190,343955,00.html).

Milan, Garth, and Donnie Bales. *Freestyle Motocross: Jump Tricks from the Pros*. 2nd edition. Osceola, WI: Motorbooks International, 2000.

Miles, Michael J. "Step Up and Freestyle Moto X." September 2000. Retrieved August 18, 2003 (http://www.off-road.com/dirtbike/sept2000/mmiles/x-games/).

INDEX

A

Adams, Nate, 49, 55, 57
Adoptante, Clifford, 45
AMA/Chevy Trucks U.S. Motocross Championship, 29
American Motorcycle Association, 29

B

Bartram, Kenny, 37, 49, 55

C

Carmichael, Ricky, 41
Carter, Jeremy, 45
Chitwood, Joey, 19, 21
Clowers, Tommy, 42, 45, 48–49
Crusty Demons of Dirt, 28–29

D

Deegan, Brian, 10, 35, 42, 44–45, 47–48, 54, 55, 56–57

E

EA Sports AMA Supercross Series, 29, 38, 50, 52
ESPN, 31, 37
extreme sports, popularity of, 30–31

F

Freeman, John, 27–28
freeriding, 25, 26
freestyle motocross (FMX)
    championships, 29
    definition of, 8–9
    start of, 26, 29
    tricks, 22–23

G

Gravity Games, 9, 32, 37, 49, 51–52

H

Hart, Carey, 23, 33, 49
Hughes, Ryan, 41

I

International Freestyle Motocross Association (IFMA), 30

K

Knievel, Evel, 18–19, 21–24, 28

M

Metal Mulisha, 10, 47–48, 54
Metzger, Mike, 32, 35, 46–47, 51
Motocross des Nations, 39–41, 42
motocross championships, 29
    tricks in, 22–23

About the Author

J. Poolos has written many books for the Rosen Publishing Group. He lives in Iowa City, Iowa.

Photo Credits

Front cover, p. 6 © Chris Polk/AP/World Wide Photos; cover (inset) © Icon Sports Media; back cover, p. 13 © Nelson Sá; p. 1 © Lonnie Timmons/AP/World Wide Photos; pp. 4, 47 © Tony Donaldson/Icon Sports Media; pp. 8–9, 50–51 © Larry Kasperek/Corbis; p. 11 © Robert Mora/Getty Images; pp. 18–19 © Bettmann/Corbis; p. 20 © AP/World Wide Photos; p. 23 © Delly Carr/AP/World Wide Photos; p. 24 © Kevin Winter/Getty Images; pp. 26–27 © Ellis Neel/AP/World Wide Photos; p. 30 © Jeff Crow/Icon Sports Media; pp. 32, 39, 40 © Diane Moore/Icon Sports Media; p. 33 © Shelly Castellano/Icon Sports Media; pp. 34–35 © Duomo/Corbis; pp. 42–43 © Jakub Mosur/AP/World Wide Photos; p. 48 © Steven Frishling/Corbis; p. 53 © Shazamm; p. 56 © Kohjiro Kinno/Corbis.

Designer: Nelson Sá; **Editor:** Christine Poolos;
Photo Researcher: Peter Tomlinson